THE BIG BOOK OF CHRISTMAS SONGS

Available for
FLUTE, CLARINET, ALTO SAX, TENOR SAX, TRUMPET, HORN, TROMBONE, VIOLIN, VIOLA, CELLO

Note: The keys in this book do not match the other wind instruments.

ISBN-13: 978-1-4234-1371-4

HAL•LEONARD®
CORPORATION
7777 W. BLUEMOUND RD. P.O. BOX 13819 MILWAUKEE, WI 53213

Visit Hal Leonard Online at
www.halleonard.com

ALL I WANT FOR CHRISTMAS IS YOU

HORN

Words and Music by MARIAH CAREY
and WALTER AFANASIEFF

A CAROLING WE GO

Music and Lyrics by
JOHNNY MARKS

ALL MY HEART THIS NIGHT REJOICES

HORN

Words and Music by JOHANN EBELING
and CATHERINE WINKWORTH

ALL THROUGH THE NIGHT

Welsh Folksong

ANGELS FROM THE REALMS OF GLORY

HORN

Words by JAMES MONTGOMERY
Music by HENRY T. SMART

ANGELS WE HAVE HEARD ON HIGH

Traditional French Carol

AS LONG AS THERE'S CHRISTMAS

from Walt Disney's BEAUTY AND THE BEAST - THE ENCHANTED CHRISTMAS

HORN

Music by RACHEL PORTMAN
Lyrics by DON BLACK

AS WITH GLADNESS MEN OF OLD

HORN

Words by WILLIAM CHATTERTON DIX
Music by CONRAD KOCHER

AULD LANG SYNE

Words by ROBERT BURNS
Traditional Scottish Melody

AWAY IN A MANGER

Traditional
Music by WILLIAM J. KIRKPATRICK

BRAZILIAN SLEIGH BELLS

HORN

By PERCY FAITH

HORN

To Coda

D.S. al Coda

CODA

BABY, IT'S COLD OUTSIDE

from the Motion Picture NEPTUNE'S DAUGHTER

HORN

By FRANK LOESSER

Moderately

BECAUSE IT'S CHRISTMAS
(For All the Children)

Horn

Music by BARRY MANILOW
Lyric by BRUCE SUSSMAN and JACK FELDMAN

AWAY IN A MANGER

Traditional
Music by JAMES R. MURRAY

BLUE CHRISTMAS

Horn

Words and Music by BILLY HAYES
and JAY JOHNSON

BREAK FORTH, O BEAUTEOUS, HEAVENLY LIGHT

Words by JOHANN RIST
Melody by JOHANN SCHOP

THE BOAR'S HEAD CAROL

HORN

Traditional English

Freely

C-H-R-I-S-T-M-A-S

Words by JENNY LOU CARSON
Music by EDDY ARNOLD

Moderately

BRING A TORCH, JEANNETTE, ISABELLA

HORN

17th Century French Provençal Carol

CAROL OF THE BELLS

Ukrainian Christmas Carol

CAROL OF THE BIRDS

Traditional Catalonian Carol

CAROLING, CAROLING

HORN

Words by WIHLA HUTSON
Music by ALFRED BURT

With a lilt

THE CHIPMUNK SONG

Words and Music by
ROSS BAGDASARIAN

Happily

A CHILD IS BORN IN BETHLEHEM

14th-Century Latin Text
Traditional Danish Melody

CHRIST WAS BORN ON CHRISTMAS DAY

Traditional

CHRISTMAS ALL ACROSS THE U.S.A.

HORN

Words and Music by
RITA ABRAMS

CHRISTMAS IN DIXIE

HORN

Words and Music by JEFFREY COOK,
TEDDY GENTRY, MARK HERNDON
and RANDY OWEN

CHRISTMAS IS ALL IN THE HEART

HORN

Words and Music by
STEVEN CURTIS CHAPMAN

Gently, in 2

To Coda ⊕   **2**   **D.S. al Coda**
(with repeat)

CODA

CHRISTMAS IS

Horn

Lyrics by SPENCE MAXWELL
Music by PERCY FAITH

Slowly

CHRISTMAS STAR

from the Twentieth Century Fox Feature Film HOME ALONE 2

Words by LESLIE BRICUSSE
Music by JOHN WILLIAMS

Slowly, gently

CHRISTMAS TIME IS HERE

from A CHARLIE BROWN CHRISTMAS

Words by LEE MENDELSON
Music by VINCE GUARALDI

CHRISTMAS IS A-COMIN'

(May God Bless You)

HORN

Words and Music by
FRANK LUTHER

THE CHRISTMAS SONG
(Chestnuts Roasting on an Open Fire)

HORN

Music and Lyric by MEL TORME
and ROBERT WELLS

Moderately

COLD DECEMBER NIGHTS

HORN

Words and Music by MICHAEL McCARY
and SHAWN STOCKMAN

THE CHRISTMAS WALTZ

Words by SAMMY CAHN
Music by JULE STYNE

Moderately, with expression

COME, THOU LONG-EXPECTED JESUS

HORN

Words by CHARLES WESLEY
Music by ROWLAND HUGH PRICHARD

COVENTRY CAROL

Words by ROBERT CROO
Traditional English Melody

DANCE OF THE SUGAR PLUM FAIRY

from THE NUTCRACKER

HORN

By PYOTR IL'YICH TCHAIKOVSKY

DECK THE HALL

Traditional Welsh Carol

DO THEY KNOW IT'S CHRISTMAS?

HORN

Words and Music by M. URE
and B. GELDOF

DON'T SAVE IT ALL FOR CHRISTMAS DAY

HORN

Words and Music by CELINE DION,
PETER ZIZZO and RIC WAKE

Slowly in one, steadily

Slower

DING DONG! MERRILY ON HIGH!

HORN

French Carol

DO YOU HEAR WHAT I HEAR

Words and Music by NOEL REGNEY
and GLORIA SHAYNE

CODA

FELIZ NAVIDAD

Music and Lyrics by
JOSÉ FELICIANO

Moderately

FROSTY THE SNOW MAN

HORN

Words and Music by STEVE NELSON
and JACK ROLLINS

THE FIRST NOEL

HORN

17th Century English Carol
Music from W. Sandys' *Christmas Carols*

THE FRIENDLY BEASTS

Traditional English Carol

FROM HEAVEN ABOVE TO EARTH I COME

Words and Music by
MARTIN LUTHER

THE GIFT

HORN

Words and Music by TOM DOUGLAS
and JIM BRICKMAN

Slow Ballad

GOING HOME FOR CHRISTMAS

HORN

Words and Music by STEVEN CURTIS CHAPMAN
and JAMES ISAAC ELLIOTT

Rhythmically and flowing

FUM, FUM, FUM

HORN

Traditional Catalonian Carol

Joyfully

GO, TELL IT ON THE MOUNTAIN

African-American Spiritual

Moderately

GOD REST YE MERRY, GENTLEMEN

HORN

19th Century English Carol

GOOD CHRISTIAN MEN, REJOICE

14th Century Latin Text
14th Century German Melody

GOOD KING WENCESLAS

Words by JOHN M. NEALE
Music from *Piae Cantiones*

GRANDMA GOT RUN OVER BY A REINDEER

HORN

Words and Music by
RANDY BROOKS

GRANDMA'S KILLER FRUITCAKE

HORN

Words and Music by ELMO SHROPSHIRE
and RITA ABRAMS

THE GREATEST GIFT OF ALL

HORN

Words and Music by
JOHN JARVIS

HARK! THE HERALD ANGELS SING

Words by CHARLES WESLEY
Music by FELIX MENDELSSOHN-BARTHOLDY

Moderately

GROWN-UP CHRISTMAS LIST

HORN

Words and Music by DAVID FOSTER
and LINDA THOMPSON-JENNER

HE IS BORN, THE HOLY CHILD
(Il est ne, le Divin Enfant)

Traditional French Carol

GREENWILLOW CHRISTMAS

HORN

By FRANK LOESSER

Moderately

HAPPY CHRISTMAS, LITTLE FRIEND

Lyrics by OSCAR HAMMERSTEIN II
Music by RICHARD RODGERS

Moderately

HAPPY HANUKKAH, MY FRIEND
(The Hanukkah Song)

HORN

Words and Music by JUSTIN WILDE
and DOUGLAS ALAN KONECKY

Moderately

HAPPY HOLIDAY

from the Motion Picture Irving Berlin's HOLIDAY INN

Words and Music by
IRVING BERLIN

HARD CANDY CHRISTMAS
from THE BEST LITTLE WHOREHOUSE IN TEXAS

HORN

Words and Music by
CAROL HALL

HE

Words by RICHARD MULLEN
Music by JACK RICHARDS

HERE COMES SANTA CLAUS
(Right Down Santa Claus Lane)

Words and Music by GENE AUTRY
and OAKLEY HALDEMAN

HAPPY XMAS
(War Is Over)

HORN

Words and Music by JOHN LENNON
and YOKO ONO

Moderately

To Coda

D.S. al Coda

CODA

HERE WE COME A-WASSAILING

HORN

Traditional

THE HOLLY AND THE IVY

18th Century English Carol

(There's No Place Like)

HOME FOR THE HOLIDAYS

HORN

Words by AL STILLMAN
Music by ROBERT ALLEN

HYMNE

HORN

By VANGELIS

66

A HOLLY JOLLY CHRISTMAS

HORN

Copyright © 1962, 1964 (Renewed 1990, 1992)
St. Nicholas Music Inc., 1619 Broadway, New York, New York 10019
All Rights Reserved

Music and Lyrics by
JOHNNY MARKS

Moderately bright

I AM SO GLAD ON CHRISTMAS EVE

Copyright © 2006 by HAL LEONARD CORPORATION
International Copyright Secured   All Rights Reserved

Words by MARIE WEXELSEN
Music by PEDER KNUDSEN

Flowing

I HEARD THE BELLS ON CHRISTMAS DAY

HORN

Words by HENRY WADSWORTH LONGFELLOW
Music by JOHN BAPTISTE CALKIN

I HEARD THE BELLS ON CHRISTMAS DAY

Words by HENRY WADSWORTH LONGFELLOW
Adapted by JOHNNY MARKS
Music by JOHNNY MARKS

I SAW THREE SHIPS

Traditional English Carol

I SAW MOMMY KISSING SANTA CLAUS

HORN

Words and Music by
TOMMIE CONNOR

I WONDER AS I WANDER

By JOHN JACOB NILES

I'M SPENDING CHRISTMAS WITH YOU

HORN

Words and Music by
TOM OCCHIPINTI

I'VE GOT MY LOVE TO KEEP ME WARM

from the 20th Century Fox Motion Picture ON THE AVENUE

HORN

Words and Music by
IRVING BERLIN

I'LL BE HOME FOR CHRISTMAS

Words and Music by KIM GANNON
and WALTER KENT

IN THE BLEAK MIDWINTER

Poem by CHRISTINA ROSSETTI
Music by GUSTAV HOLST

IT MUST HAVE BEEN THE MISTLETOE
(Our First Christmas)

HORN

By JUSTIN WILDE
and DOUG KONECKY

IT CAME UPON THE MIDNIGHT CLEAR

Words by EDMUND HAMILTON SEARS
Music by RICHARD STORRS WILLIS

IT'S BEGINNING TO LOOK LIKE CHRISTMAS

HORN

By MEREDITH WILLSON

IT'S JUST ANOTHER NEW YEAR'S EVE

Horn

Lyric by MARTY PANZER
Music by BARRY MANILOW

IT'S CHRISTMAS TIME ALL OVER THE WORLD

HORN

Words and Music by
HUGH MARTIN

Fast and gaily

JESUS HOLY, BORN SO LOWLY

Traditional Polish

JESU, JOY OF MAN'S DESIRING

HORN

By JOHANN SEBASTIAN BACH

JINGLE BELLS

HORN

Words and Music by
J. PIERPONT

JINGLE, JINGLE, JINGLE

Music and Lyrics by
JOHNNY MARKS

JOLLY OLD ST. NICHOLAS

Traditional 19th Century American Carol

JINGLE-BELL ROCK

HORN

Words and Music by JOE BEAL
and JIM BOOTHE

Moderately, with a Rock beat

LET'S HAVE AN OLD FASHIONED CHRISTMAS

HORN

Lyric by LARRY CONLEY
Music by JOE SOLOMON

LAST CHRISTMAS

HORN

Words and Music by
GEORGE MICHAEL

JOY TO THE WORLD

Words by ISAAC WATTS
Music by GEORGE FRIDERIC HANDEL

Brightly

mf

(Everybody's Waitin' For)
THE MAN WITH THE BAG

Horn

Words and Music by HAROLD STANLEY,
IRVING TAYLOR and DUDLEY BROOKS

LET IT SNOW! LET IT SNOW! LET IT SNOW!

Words by SAMMY CAHN
Music by JULE STYNE

THE LAST MONTH OF THE YEAR
(What Month Was Jesus Born In?)

HORN

Words and Music by VERA HALL
Adapted and Arranged by RUBY PICKENS TARTT
and ALAN LOMAX

LITTLE SAINT NICK

Words and Music by BRIAN WILSON
and MIKE LOVE

LO, HOW A ROSE E'ER BLOOMING

15th Century German Carol
Music from *Alte Catholische Geistliche Kirchengesang*

MARCH OF THE THREE KINGS

HORN

Words by M. L. HOHMAN
Traditional French Melody

A MARSHMALLOW WORLD

HORN

Words by CARL SIGMAN
Music by PETER DE ROSE

MASTERS IN THIS HALL

HORN

Traditional English

MELE KALIKIMAKA

Words and Music by
ALEX ANDERSON

MERRY CHRISTMAS, BABY

HORN

Words and Music by LOU BAXTER
and JOHNNY MOORE

MERRY CHRISTMAS, DARLING

HORN

Words and Music by RICHARD CARPENTER
and FRANK POOLER

MERRY CHRISTMAS, MERRY CHRISTMAS

from the Twentieth Century Fox Feature Film HOME ALONE 2

HORN

Words by LESLIE BRICUSSE
Music by JOHN WILLIAMS

MISS YOU MOST AT CHRISTMAS TIME

Horn

Words and Music by MARIAH CAREY
and WALTER AFANASIEFF

THE MERRY CHRISTMAS POLKA

Words by PAUL FRANCIS WEBSTER
Music by SONNY BURKE

MISTER SANTA

HORN

Words and Music by
PAT BALLARD

A MERRY, MERRY CHRISTMAS TO YOU

Music and Lyrics by
JOHNNY MARKS

MISTLETOE AND HOLLY

Words and Music by FRANK SINATRA,
DOK STANFORD and HENRY W. SANICOLA

THE MOST WONDERFUL DAY OF THE YEAR

HORN

Music and Lyrics by
JOHNNY MARKS

THE NIGHT BEFORE CHRISTMAS SONG

Music by JOHNNY MARKS
Lyrics adapted by JOHNNY MARKS
from Clement Moore's Poem

THE MOST WONDERFUL TIME OF THE YEAR

HORN

Words and Music by EDDIE POLA
and GEORGE WYLE

MY FAVORITE THINGS
from THE SOUND OF MUSIC

HORN

Lyrics by OSCAR HAMMERSTEIN II
Music by RICHARD RODGERS

MY ONLY WISH THIS YEAR

HORN

Words and Music by BRIAN KIERULF
and JOSHUA SCHWARTZ

Fast Shuffle

O CHRISTMAS TREE

Traditional German Carol

O COME, ALL YE FAITHFUL
(Adeste Fideles)

HORN

Words and Music by JOHN FRANCIS WADE
Latin words translated by FREDERICK OAKELEY

NUTTIN' FOR CHRISTMAS

Words and Music by ROY BENNETT
and SID TEPPER

O COME, LITTLE CHILDREN

Words by C. VON SCHMIDT
Music by J.P.A. SCHULZ

Quietly

108

O COME, O COME IMMANUEL

HORN

Plainsong, 13th Century

O LITTLE TOWN OF BETHLEHEM

Words by PHILLIPS BROOKS
Music by LEWIS H. REDNER

O SANCTISSIMA

Sicilian Carol

O HOLY NIGHT

HORN

French words by PLACIDE CAPPEAU
English words by JOHN S. DWIGHT
Music by ADOLPHE ADAM

Moderately

OF THE FATHER'S LOVE BEGOTTEN

Words by AURELIUS C. PRUDENTIUS
13th Century Plainsong

Freely

ON CHRISTMAS NIGHT

HORN

Sussex Carol

OLD TOY TRAINS

Words and Music by
ROGER MILLER

PRETTY PAPER

Words and Music by
WILLIE NELSON

PLEASE COME HOME FOR CHRISTMAS

HORN

Words and Music by CHARLES BROWN
and GENE REDD

Moderately

ONCE IN ROYAL DAVID'S CITY

Words by CECIL F. ALEXANDER
Music by HENRY J. GAUNTLETT

PAT-A-PAN
(Willie, Take Your Little Drum)

HORN

Words and Music by
BERNARD DE LA MONNOYE

RISE UP, SHEPHERD, AND FOLLOW

African-American Spiritual

ROCKIN' AROUND THE CHRISTMAS TREE

HORN

Music and Lyrics by
JOHNNY MARKS

Moderate Rock

RUDOLPH THE RED-NOSED REINDEER

HORN

Music and Lyrics by
JOHNNY MARKS

SANTA BABY

HORN

By JOAN JAVITS,
PHIL SPRINGER and TONY SPRINGER

SANTA CLAUS IS BACK IN TOWN

HORN

Words and Music by JERRY LEIBER
and MIKE STOLLER

SANTA CLAUS IS COMIN' TO TOWN

Words by HAVEN GILLESPIE
Music by J. FRED COOTS

SHAKE ME I RATTLE
(Squeeze Me I Cry)

Words and Music by HAL HACKADY
and CHARLES NAYLOR

Moderately slow

SANTA, BRING MY BABY BACK
(To Me)

HORN

Words and Music by CLAUDE DeMETRUIS
and AARON SCHROEDER

SHEPHERDS, SHAKE OFF YOUR DROWSY SLEEP

HORN

Traditional French Carol

With energy

SILVER AND GOLD

Music and Lyrics by
JOHNNY MARKS

Slowly and expressively

1.

2.

SILENT NIGHT

HORN

Words by JOSEPH MOHR
Translated by JOHN F. YOUNG
Music by FRANZ X. GRUBER

SILVER BELLS

from the Paramount Picture THE LEMON DROP KID

Words and Music by JAY LIVINGSTON
and RAY EVANS

SING WE NOW OF CHRISTMAS

HORN

Traditional French Carol

SNOWFALL

Lyrics by RUTH THORNHILL
Music by CLAUDE THORNHILL

SOME THINGS FOR CHRISTMAS
(A Snake, Some Mice, Some Glue and a Hole Too)

HORN

Lyric by JACQUELYN REINACH and JOAN LAMPORT
Music by JACQUELYN REINACH

SOME CHILDREN SEE HIM

Lyric by WIHLA HUTSON
Music by ALFRED BURT

SPECIAL GIFT

Horn

Words and Music by MYRON DAVIS
and STANLEY BROWN

SOMEWHERE IN MY MEMORY

from the Twentieth Century Fox Motion Picture HOME ALONE

Words by LESLIE BRICUSSE
Music by JOHN WILLIAMS

Gently and with simplicity

THE STAR CAROL

HORN

Lyric by WIHLA HUTSON
Music by ALFRED BURT

Tenderly, with much expression

SUZY SNOWFLAKE

Words and Music by SID TEPPER
and ROY BENNETT

Moderately

TENNESSEE CHRISTMAS

Horn

Words and Music by AMY GRANT
and GARY CHAPMAN

STILL, STILL, STILL

HORN

Salzburg Melody, c.1819
Traditional Austrian Text

THAT CHRISTMAS FEELING

Words and Music by BENNIE BENJAMIN
and GEORGE WEISS

THIS CHRISTMAS

Horn

Words and Music by DONNY HATHAWAY
and NADINE McKINNOR

TOYLAND

Words by GLEN MacDONOUGH
Music by VICTOR HERBERT

THE TWELVE DAYS OF CHRISTMAS

Traditional English Carol

*These bars are played a different number of times for each verse.

UP ON THE HOUSETOP

HORN

Words and Music by
B.R. HANDY

WATCHMAN, TELL US OF THE NIGHT

Traditional

WE NEED A LITTLE CHRISTMAS

from MAME

HORN

Music and Lyric by
JERRY HERMAN

WE THREE KINGS OF ORIENT ARE

HORN

Words and Music by
JOHN H. HOPKINS, JR.

WE WISH YOU A MERRY CHRISTMAS

Traditional English Folksong

WEXFORD CAROL

HORN

Traditional Irish Carol

WHAT CHILD IS THIS?

Words by WILLIAM C. DIX
16th Century English Melody

WHAT ARE YOU DOING NEW YEAR'S EVE?

HORN

By FRANK LOESSER

Slowly and sentimentally

WHO WOULD IMAGINE A KING

from the Touchstone Motion Picture THE PREACHER'S WIFE

HORN

Words and Music by MERVYN WARREN
and HALLERIN HILTON HILL

Gentle Waltz

THE WHITE WORLD OF WINTER

Words by MITCHELL PARISH
Music by HOAGY CARMICHAEL

Moderately, with a lift

WONDERFUL CHRISTMASTIME

HORN

Words and Music by
PAUL McCARTNEY

YOU'RE ALL I WANT FOR CHRISTMAS

Words and Music by GLEN MOORE
and SEGER ELLIS

Slowly and evenly

YOU DON'T HAVE TO BE ALONE

HORN

Words and Music by VEIT RENN,
JOSHUA CHASEZ and DAVID NICOLL

WHEN CHRISTMAS MORN IS DAWNING

Traditional Swedish

WHEN SANTA CLAUS GETS YOUR LETTER

HORN

Music and Lyrics by
JOHNNY MARKS